THE GUNP
INDUS1

Glenys Crocker

Gunpowder workers at Chilworth, Surrey, about 1913. The works operated around the clock, and the men worked twelve-hour shifts. They were searched on arrival and were issued with working clothes without pockets to guard against dangerous articles being brought on site. The tramlines are part of a 2 foot 7¹/₂ inch (800 mm) gauge track, which, together with punts on the millstream, provided transport around the works.

Shire Publications

CONTENTS

ACKNOWLEDGEMENTS

The author wishes to thank the many people whose help, interest and hospitality have made the preparation of this book a pleasure to undertake, and especially members of the Gunpowder Mills Study Group for information and valuable discussions. Particular thanks are due to the Faversham Society and the Waltham Abbey Royal Gunpowder Mills Project for help with illustrations; to Alan Crocker for redrawing the line illustrations on pages 14 (top), 18 (all) and 20 (top), which are based on drawings in an original notebook in private ownership and in another version in the Kent Archives Office (U269 0187/1); and to Gareth Crocker for processing and printing the author's photographs.

Illustrations are acknowledged as follows: British Library, pages 16-17 (top); reproduced by permission of the Governing Body of Christ Church, Oxford (MS92, fol. 70v.), page 3; Glenys Crocker, page 27 (bottom), 28 (all), 29, 30 (bottom) and front cover; Bryan Earl, page 9; the Faversham Society, page 23 (both); A. Hammond, page 25; Hastings Museum, page 20 (centre); Illustrated London News Picture Library, page 24; Cadbury Lamb, page 27 (top); Langdale Leisure Limited, page 22; London Borough of Hounslow Library Services, page 7; Alice Palmer, page 21 (labels); Dr Daphne Pochin-Mould and Cork County Council, page 26; Public Record Office, page 5 (SP16.361) and 15 (top) (M.P.II.15); Jim Puddick, page 1; Roslin Local History Society, page 21 (plaque); the Royal Commission on the Ancient and Historical Monuments of Scotland, page 15 (bottom); Trustees of the Science Museum, London, pages 4, 12 (bottom), 14 (bottom); Surrey History Centre (G.132/1), page 6; Waltham Abbey Royal Gunpowder Mills Project, pages 10, 11, 13 (top), 19 (bottom), 30 (top).

Cover: *A mortar for testing gunpowder at Powdermills, Two Bridges, Devon, where blasting powder was made in the nineteenth century. The mortar has an 8 inch (260 mm) bore.*

British Library Cataloguing in Publication Data: Crocker, Glenys The gunpowder industry. – 2nd ed. – (Shire album; no.160) 1. Gunpowder industry – Great Britain – History I. Title 338.4'7'66226'0941'09 ISBN 0 7478 0393 5.

Published in 2002 by Shire Publications Ltd, Cromwell House, Church Street, Princes Risborough, Buckinghamshire HP27 9AA, UK. (Website: www.shirebooks.co.uk)
Copyright © 1986 and 1999 by Glenys Crocker. First published 1986. Second edition 1999; reprinted 2002. Shire Album 160. ISBN 0 7478 0393 5.
Glenys Crocker is hereby identified as the author of this work in accordance with Section 77 of the Copyright, Designs and Patents Act 1988.

Printed in Great Britain by CIT Printing Services Ltd, Press Buildings, Merlins Bridge, Haverfordwest, Pembrokeshire SA61 1XF.

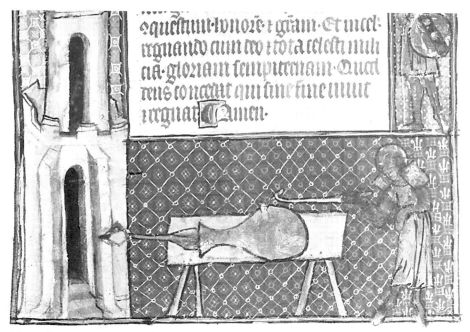

The earliest representation of a gun, from the manuscript of Walter de Milemete, 1326.

THE INVENTION OF GUNPOWDER

Gunpowder is a mixture of saltpetre, charcoal and sulphur, usually in the proportions of 75:15:10. The saltpetre, or potassium nitrate, supplies oxygen, and the other constituents provide fuel, the sulphur serving to inflame at a relatively low temperature. The formula has varied, and in general the earlier compositions contained less nitrate.

The early developments took place in China, where deflagrating mixtures of the three ingredients were known to alchemists by the ninth century AD. The first known written formula appeared in the *Wu Ching Tsung Yao,* a treatise on military techniques that was completed in 1044. By that time the Chinese were using saltpetre mixtures of low nitrate content in simple bombs and grenades and in flame throwers made from hollow stems of bamboo. The next step was to shoot projectiles, such as fragments of metal and arrows, from a tube, and this was followed in about 1280 by the true gun, with a metal barrel and a projectile that closely fitted the muzzle.

The West had a wide range of incendiary devices that required atmospheric oxygen in which to burn, including the distilled petroleum product known as 'Greek fire', which was introduced in Byzantium in the seventh century AD. The use of saltpetre represented a completely different development, which was introduced to Europe from China via the Arab world in the first half of the thirteenth century.

A method of purifying saltpetre was described by the Franciscan Roger Bacon, writing in about the year 1260. Bacon also gave a recipe for 'thunder and lightning' but wrote it in the form of an anagram, for fear of its misappropriation by the unwise.

3

A saltpetre works in central Europe, from a treatise by Lazarus Ercker, 1580. Nitrous earth is scraped from the beds (C), and saltpetre is extracted in solution in the leaching house (A). Wood ashes, which contain potassium carbonate, were added to remove calcium salts. In the boiling house (B) the liquor is boiled down and run into vats, where it cools and the saltpetre crystallises. The product was further refined by the powder makers.

The favoured interpretation of the Latin text specifies seven parts of saltpetre to five of charcoal and five of sulphur.

Bacon's contemporary Albertus Magnus gave the corresponding proportions as 6:2:1 and described the making of firecrackers and rockets. The ingredients were to be finely ground on a marble slab and enclosed in paper cases. These were to be long, thin and well filled for 'flying fire' and short, thick and half-filled for 'thunder'. The same instructions appear, as a late addition made in about 1300, in the *Book of Fires for the Burning of Enemies,* a collection of recipes attributed to Marcus Graecus.

Thirteenth-century writers in the West recognised only the explosive and pyrotechnic properties of saltpetre mixtures, and it was not until the fourteenth century that the propellent form, gunpowder, was developed in Europe. The earliest guns appear to have been bottle-shaped and to have used arrows as projectiles. By 1350 small cannon were becoming fairly common, and spherical projectiles were in use. From then onwards, firearms developed more rapidly in Europe than in the Far East, but their role in battle did not become decisive until after the end of the middle ages.

A claim for compensation for damage caused by digging for saltpetre, from 'The Articles of Christopher Wren, Deane of Windsor and Rector of Knoile Epicopi Wiltes against Thomas Thornhill, Salt Peter Man, for undermining and throwing downe the Pidgeon House of the said Rectory ...' (1636). The pigeon house of Christopher Wren, who was the father of the famous architect of the same name, had been damaged on two occasions, the first eight years previously.

SALTPETRE

Potassium nitrate forms naturally in warm climates that have a regular dry season, such as occurs in India, North Africa and parts of eastern and southern Europe. In moist conditions organic matter decays through the action of certain bacteria, and nitrates are formed which combine with potassium compounds to give potassium nitrate in solution. In a subsequent hot, dry season, this rises to the surface of the soil, where the water evaporates, leaving a deposit of salts on the ground.

Saltpetre from India came into Europe through Venice in the middle ages, but there was another, minor source closer at hand. An efflorescence was found to occur on walls, such as those of stables and outbuildings, which were built of earth and manure and came into contact with urine. These deposits were collected by scraping, and in the late fourteenth century in central Europe a method was discovered of creating the conditions for their formation in artificial nitre beds. The practice was not understood in England until considerably later.

Gunpowder was made in England from imported ingredients from the fourteenth century onwards, and much ready-made powder was purchased abroad. An urgent need for an independent supply arose during the reign of Elizabeth I, when relations with Spain grew hostile, and in 1561 instructions 'for making saltpetre to growe' were purchased from a German captain, Gerrard Honrick, for the sum of £300.

The following ingredients were required: 'Fyrst black earth the blacker the better. The next is Urine, namely of those persons whiche drink either wyne or strong bears. Then Dong specially of those horses, which be fed with ootes, and be always kept in the stables. The fourth is Lyme made of plaster of Parys. The Lyme whiche is made of Oyster Shellis is the best...' The instructions continue over four closely written pages. Briefly, the heap was turned at intervals over a period of months until sufficient salts had formed. These were extracted in solution, and the resulting liquor was boiled down and allowed to cool so that crystals of saltpetre precipitated.

Until the East India Company established a steady import trade in Indian saltpetre in the second half of the seventeenth century, the collection of sufficient manure presented a perennial problem. Saltpetre men were therefore appointed who had the right to enter and dig in buildings such as dovehouses and stables. Under James I a system of weekly quotas was introduced, and, although provision was made for the repair of damage and exemption of inhabited dwellings, in practice the efforts of the collectors to fulfil their obligations resulted in many grievances. When the import trade with the East developed it was dominated by England and the Netherlands, and in other countries the burden of collection remained. In France, for example, the *sâlpetriers* had extensive rights, which continued to cause great resentment until the revolution of 1789.

In the nineteenth century a method was developed, using potassium chloride, of manufacturing potassium nitrate from sodium nitrate or Chile saltpetre, which was readily available from South America and was cheaper than the Indian variety.

Part of a letter from William Tinkler, powder maker, of Chilworth, Surrey, to a customer in Scotland, 1790. 'Above you have Invoice for Dundee per the Countess of Kennoul Capt Wishart Amount £7-2-6 your order for Powder for Saltcoats shall ship in first Vessel, but you have not mentioned whether you wish to have the Spanish White shipped with it. I have now got the letter I mentioned the 27th Ult that was recd from the Powder makers at Kendale wherein they say they have lost their Business in Scotland in a great degree except a trifle sold by John Laird & Co Greenock & among the Americans Merchants where they have no dispute about the price.' Orders were supplied from the firm's central magazine at Barking Creek on the Thames estuary. 'Spanish White' was a form of talc used for cleaning. Competition was increasing in the late eighteenth century as new mills were being set up in the north of England and Scotland. Prices were agreed by the powder makers after the East India Company's sale of saltpetre in March and September, and there had been a complaint about underselling.

'Mr Hill's Gunpowder Mills on Hounslow Heath', about 1800. The mills, which operated from the seventeenth century until 1926, were situated on the river Crane in the area occupied by the modern Crane Park in west London. The firm of Curtis's & Harvey's, which took over many factories throughout Britain in the course of the nineteenth century, was established at the site in 1820. The mills in the illustration are water-powered, and the chimneys are associated with drying kilns and saltpetre refining.

THE HISTORY OF THE GUNPOWDER INDUSTRY

The first recorded use of gunpowder by English soldiers was at the battle of Crecy in 1346, during the Hundred Years War with France, and accounts from the Tower of London show that powder was by then being made in England.

The early makers did not have sophisticated plant but made relatively small quantities of powder by hand with a pestle and mortar. Much of the manufacture was carried out by gunners in the arsenals, and some powder was made in the field as it was needed because the early product tended to separate into its constituent ingredients during transit.

Water-driven powder mills are known in Britain from the sixteenth century onwards. One existed on the Thames at Rotherhithe by 1543, but there is a lack of firm evidence for other early sites. Several were probably built after 1560, for in that year the government was advised that 'four or six' were needed, and in 1561 instructions for making saltpetre were purchased.

The supply of powder was, however, very inadequate when the Spanish Armada attempted to invade England in 1588. It was therefore decided to introduce a proper system of contracting with manufacturers, and, beginning in 1589, certain makers were licensed by royal letters patent. The Evelyn family of Tolworth and later of Godstone and Wotton in Surrey then began a long period of prominence in the industry, as holders of appointments under Elizabeth I and of the monopoly introduced by her successor. In 1621 James I appointed the Lords of the Admiralty as Commissioners for Saltpetre and Gunpowder. The kingdom was divided into districts for the collection of saltpetre, and a series of three-year contracts was made with John Evelyn to manufacture gunpowder. The contract of 1621 was for 120 lasts, of 144 tons, annually, to be delivered to the Tower of London, which held the main gunpowder store. This quantity was doubled in the contract of 1624. Two-thirds of the powder was for the king's stores, and the rest was assigned to merchant seamen and other private subjects.

Although the industry was in principle a monopoly, several other factories were operating, some under licence. Illicit powder making was carried on in Southwark and Lambeth, in Sussex, Devon and with notable persistence in Bristol, whose seaport provided a ready market. Some Bristol makers were also on occasion licensed to make powder for local shipping.

The East India Company, which had received its charter in 1600, was authorised to manufacture powder for its own use and set up mills at Chilworth in Surrey in 1626. The venture lasted only a few years, but the mills continued to operate, and their proprietors were granted the monopoly in 1636.

The monopoly was abolished by the Long Parliament in 1641, on the eve of the Civil War. After the restoration of the monarchy, a sole powder maker was again appointed who delegated his authority to several manufacturers, but in 1664 the Board of Ordnance was placed in control. An increase in the demand for powder arose from the Dutch wars, from the 1650s onwards, and the War of the Spanish Succession in the early eighteenth century. Surrey continued for a time to be the largest producer, but the industry began to expand in other parts of south-east England.

Most powder mills were situated at a safe but convenient distance from London, where the Ordnance was based. They were typically built on tributaries of the Thames, which provided water power for the various manufacturing processes and transport for the powder and raw materials. There were major centres of production in the Lea valley in Essex, where about eight mills, including the important Waltham Abbey factory, were operating at various dates, at Faversham in Kent and at Bedfont and Hounslow in Middlesex. There were also new developments in Surrey and around the town of Battle in East Sussex. In Ireland, a water-powered mill had been established near Dublin in the 1590s, and others were started in the vicinity in the eighteenth century.

The Ordnance Board was the industry's main customer, but there was also a large market for gunpowder for merchant shipping, for both defence and trade. London was the major port, but in the eighteenth century first Bristol and then Liverpool developed as ports of the triangular slave trade with West Africa and the Americas. Powder mills were established near both, at Woolley in Somerset in the 1720s and at Thelwall in Cheshire in 1758.

The Somerset mills also supplied blasting powder to local coal and lead mines and to the mines of Wales and Cornwall. Blasting with gunpowder spread in Europe after 1627, when it was recorded in Hungary, and in England from 1665 onwards. Existing mills in south-east England began supplying the mines, but in due course a gunpowder industry became established in other parts of Britain. The first of an important group of mills in southern Cumbria was started at Sedgwick near Kendal in 1764. The industry spread to the Edinburgh area and to County Cork in Ireland in the late eighteenth century, to Derbyshire in 1801 and Cornwall in 1809, and there were new developments in south-east England, for example in 1811 at Tonbridge in Kent.

Although particular markets dominated the industry in certain areas, specialisation was not always exclusive, and many firms made a wide range of products, from blasting powder, which was the crudest type, to fine sporting grades. However, the involvement of Quaker entrepreneurs in Cornwall shows that the industry there was far removed from military concerns. One important speciality was the fine sporting powder known as 'Battle' powder, which was made in Sussex.

Some gunpowder was used to manufacture fireworks. Crackers and rockets predated the propellent form of gunpowder, and later, when many new materials were introduced for special pyrotechnic effects, gunpowder continued to be used to activate the display and to give extra fierceness. Fireworks were in principle made illegal in 1697, and although in practice their use was not prevented – indeed, the authorities themselves commissioned displays on occasions of public rejoicing – a properly regulated industry could not develop until it was legitimised by the Explosives Act of 1860.

In the military sector, the government ceased to rely on private manufacturers when it acquired the mills at Faversham in 1759, followed by Waltham Abbey in 1787 and Ballincollig in County Cork in 1804. The success of the government enterprise was in large measure due to Major William Congreve, Comptroller of the Royal Laboratory, who was created Baronet in 1812. Congreve's son William succeeded to his title and office in 1814.

The younger Congreve was the author of several inventions including the military rocket, which he introduced in 1805. Congreve rockets were based on weapons used against the British in India in the late eighteenth century. They were used in the Napoleonic Wars and most famously in the British attack on Fort McHenry in Maryland in 1814, which inspired the line 'the rockets' red glare' in the United States' national anthem. They became obsolete as weapons after about 1850 because of improvements in artillery but continued to be used for flares and ship rescue.

Demand for military powder increased greatly during the Napoleonic Wars and fell afterwards. The Waltham Abbey mills made over 22,000 barrels of powder in 1813 but only one thousand each year following the final defeat of Bonaparte, and their workforce fell from 250 in 1813 to thirty-four in 1822. The government sold the Faversham factory in 1825 and the Ballincollig works in 1834, retaining only Waltham Abbey as a royal factory.

Some markets were lost in the early nineteenth century as a gunpowder industry started in America, and the Woolley mills closed at this time. However, new markets

The Bickford Smith factory at Tuckingmill, Cornwall, where William Bickford invented his miner's safety fuse in 1831. The picture, from a dsiplay of the 1880s, shows working copper and tin mines in the distance.

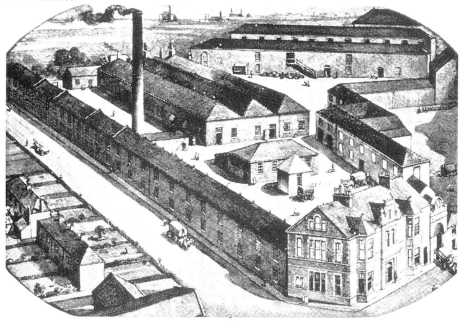

The saltpetre refinery at the Royal Gunpowder Mills, Waltham Abbey, 1895. 'Grough' saltpetre was dissolved in water in 500 gallon (2300 litre) coppers, boiled, skimmed and run through filter bags into the cooling vessels shown here. The solution was agitated as it cooled so that small pure crystals formed. These are being raked out on to drainers before being transferred to washing vats. The liquors produced at each stage were retained and recycled.

began to open up through industrial and civil engineering developments in Britain and abroad, particularly in the expanding colonies, which needed powder for both firearms and blasting.

A new industry based on gunpowder was launched by the invention of the miner's safety fuse in 1805 by William Bickford of Tuckingmill in Cornwall. Bickford was concerned to reduce the toll of accidents caused by crude and unpredictable fuses made from reeds and goose quills. Together with a local miner, Thomas Davey, he developed a textile fibre fuse with a uniform core of powder that burnt at a determinate rate. The fuse was made in a rope walk, the powder being trickled into a bundle of fibres as these were being twisted. More fibres were wound around in the opposite direction, to counter the twist, and a varnish of tar and resin was applied.

Bickford fuse soon acquired a worldwide market, and factories were opened in several countries for its manufacture. The product was adapted for use in different climatic conditions and for special purposes such as underwater blasting. Another type of fuse was developed, notably by the Cornish firm of Tangye, in which the powder was contained in a lead or composition pipe. The manufacture of fuse continued in Cornwall until the 1960s, long outlasting the traditional gunpowder industry in the county.

New gunpowder mills were started in the mid nineteenth century in the west of Scotland, Wales, Devon, Cornwall and the Lake District. Many technical improvements were made, but at the same time a new high explosives industry based on more modern chemical technology was making rapid progress. Gunpowder, or black powder as it became called, to distinguish it from newer products, eventually became obsolete for most purposes. Before describing these developments, it is necessary to explain how it was made.

Ladling liquid sulphur into wooden tubs from the receiving pot of the distilling plant at Waltham Abbey, 1895.

THE MANUFACTURE OF BLACK POWDER

The saltpetre and sulphur were refined, and wood was burned for charcoal. The ingredients were pulverised, weighed, mixed and then incorporated by mechanically grinding and crushing them together into an intimate mixture known as mill cake. This was broken down, pressed into hard slate-like sheets of press cake, corned (formed into grains), dusted, glazed and finally dried.

Powder that had deteriorated in storage or at sea could be reworked, and government contracts were issued for the 'repair' of old powder as well as for the supply of new.

PREPARATION

The crude or 'grough' saltpetre, which was imported or made in local nitre beds, was dissolved in water, boiled and recrystallised. Sulphur, which was imported from Italy and Sicily, was distilled.

Charcoal was the variable factor, and its preparation involved selection of the wood and control of the burning process. Charcoal made by traditional methods, in stacks, was impure and uneven, so a new method of distilling wood in sealed retorts was developed in the late eighteenth century. Coppices were planted around powder mills to supply wood. The preferred trees were alder, willow and alder buckthorn, which was commonly known in England as 'dogwood', and juniper was used locally in the Lake District.

Saltpetre could be used straight from the refinery, but the charcoal and sulphur were pulverised under stone edge runners. In the nineteenth century machines similar to giant coffee grinders were introduced for pulverising charcoal. The powdered ingredients were each sieved to ensure uniformity and to remove any gritty particles that might cause an explosion during manufacture.

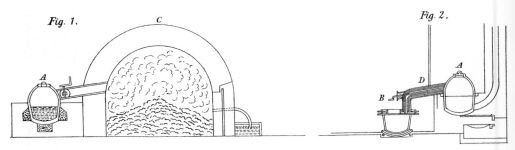

Sulphur-refining apparatus, late nineteenth century. Grough sulphur is heated in the melting pot (A), and the initial yellow vapour is led into the subliming chamber (C), where it falls down as flowers of sulphur. This was not used in the manufacture of gunpowder but was returned to the melting pot. As heating continues, the subsequent brown vapour flows through the cold water jacket (D) to condense in the receiving pot (B). From Wardell's 'Handbook of Gunpowder and Guncotton', 1888.

The saltpetre, charcoal and sulphur were next weighed out in the required proportions. By the early nineteenth century these had become generally established at 75:15:10, but with some variation in different countries and for different purposes, for example 70:15:15 for blasting powder. The ingredients were then mixed in a revolving drum to produce the 'green charge' for the incorporating mills.

INCORPORATING

The early method of incorporating was by pestle and mortar, worked originally by hand and later by a horse-driven or water-powered camshaft. Incorporating mills with stone edge runners were introduced in Britain in the late seventeenth century and widely adopted in the eighteenth. In some countries, particularly France and North America, pestle mills continued to be preferred until well into the nineteenth century, but in 1772 they were made illegal in Great Britain on grounds of safety, except at mills in Sussex that made fine 'Battle' powder for fowling.

The traditional method of charcoal burning, from Biringuccio's 'Pirotechnia', 1559.

The charge was moistened from time to time during incorporation, which took about two hours for blasting powder and eight hours or more for fine sporting grades. Production was continuous when necessary, with the workforce operating a shift system.

In the nineteenth century steam engines and later water turbines were introduced to drive machinery. Improvements to the design of incorporating mills enabled a larger charge to be processed, and the legal limit was increased from 40 pounds (18 kg) in 1772 to 60 pounds (27 kg) in 1860, 80 pounds (36 kg) in the 1880s and 250 pounds (113 kg) in the 1930s.

BREAKING DOWN

The mill cake, which contained a proportion of moisture ranging from one to six per cent according to the type of powder, was taken off the bed of the incorporating mill

Making cylinder charcoal at Waltham Abbey, 1895. The charring of wood in airtight cylinders, from which the by-products of combustion were extracted, was developed for the government factories in the late eighteenth century by Richard Watson, Professor of Chemistry at Cambridge and absentee Bishop of Llandaff.

Diagram of charcoal cylinders from Parkes's 'Chemical Essays', 1815, showing the arrangement of flues and the barrels for collecting tar and pyroligneous acid.

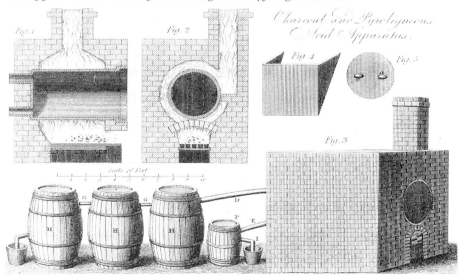

A horse-driven crushing mill with edge runners at the Royal Gunpowder Mills, Faversham, 1796. The drawing shows the crushing of saltpetre that had been cast into round cakes. Similar equipment was used for pulverising charcoal and sulphur before mixing the charge for the incorporating mills.

Pestle incorporating mills, from Diderot's 'Encyclopédie', 1762-77. Rows of stamps are operated by a camshaft. Pestle mills were in general made illegal in Britain in 1772 but survived into the nineteenth century in North America and some European countries.

14

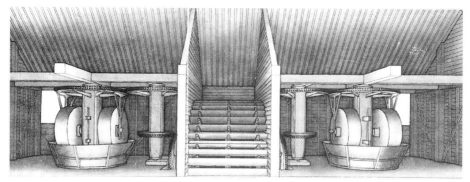

Edge-runner incorporating mills at Waltham Abbey, 1830, from a drawing by Frederick Drayson. The drawing shows a typical construction of a pair of mills driven by a central waterwheel and geared from above. Later mills, particularly those driven by steam, were geared from beneath so that the machinery was less vulnerable to destruction in an explosion. The bedstone is enclosed in a curb to contain the charge, which weighed 40 pounds (18 kg). The stone edge runners are mounted asymmetrically on the shaft and are preceded by ploughs that push the charge into their path to give a combined crushing, grinding and mixing action. In the late nineteenth century incorporating mills were made of iron, and the edge runners were suspended slightly above the bed instead of resting upon it, allowing a larger charge to be processed safely.

An underdriven, electrically powered iron incorporating mill with suspended runners at Ardeer in Ayrshire. The Ardeer factory was established by Nobel's British Dynamite Company in 1872, and black powder production was moved there by ICI in the 1930s. By then the authorised mill charge was 250 pounds (113 kg). (Crown Copyright: Royal Commission on the Ancient and Historical Monuments of Scotland)

To John Walton Eſqr Proprietor of theſe Mills this Plate is

R. Hale delin 1735.

Above: *Powder mills at Waltham Abbey, Essex, in 1735, from John Farmer's 'History'. From the right the buildings are: 1 horse mill; 2 corning and glazing engine; 3-5 three horse mills; 6 stables; 7 coal (charcoal) mill and composition house; 8 carpenters' and millwrights' workhouse; 9 clerk's counting house and watch house; 10 loading house; 11-12 two stamping mills; 13-14 two dumb mills; 15 charging house; 16 old composition house; 17 store house; 18 dusting house; 19 little stove; 20 three sun stoves or drying leads; 21 great stove. The drawing shows the transition from stamping or pestle mills to incorporating mills with edge runners, here described as 'dumb mills' because of their quiet operation. The mills were situated on the river Lea, which provided transport to the Thames as well as water power. The earliest clear evidence for gunpowder manufacture at Waltham Abbey dates from 1665, during the Second Dutch War, although there were earlier powder mills at nearby Sewardstone and on the Lea nearer London. In 1787 the Waltham Abbey Mills were taken over by the government and operated as the Royal Gunpowder Factory until 1945. After the Second World War this became a government research establishment, which closed in 1991. Most of the site is being developed as a public amenity, nature reserve and museum of the explosives industry.*

with wooden implements. The next stage involved crushing it into a convenient form for loading into the press. In the nineteenth century it was reduced to meal by passing it between pairs of revolving gunmetal rollers in a breaking-down machine.

PRESSING AND CORNING

Presses became necessary, to increase the density of the mill cake, when pestle mills were replaced by incorporating mills with edge runners.

Corning was an earlier introduction. Originally gunpowder was simply incorporated and dried, but in this form it did not explode consistently and the ingredients tended to separate out again. The practice therefore began in the sixteenth century of forcing it through punched parchment sieves to form 'corn powder'. The loose type then became known as serpentine powder, after guns of the period. As with incorporating,

humbly dedicated by his Obedient humble Servant J. Farmer

Jn⁽ᵒ⁾ Mynair Sculp

Below: *A breaking-down machine for crushing mill cake for the press, from Wardell's 'Handbook of Gunpowder and Guncotton', 1888.*

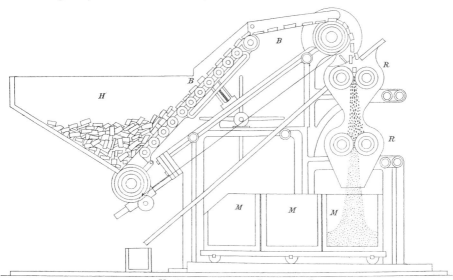

H . Hopper, B. Endless Band, R. Rollers.
M. Boxes to receive meal.

Above: *A gunpowder screw press at Faversham, 1796. Mill cake was broken up and placed in layers between the copper plates of the press on the right. It was compacted to about half its original thickness to form slabs of hard press cake about 1/2 inch (13 mm) thick. These were removed with copper utensils, broken into small pieces with wooden mallets and taken to the corning machine on the left. Pressing was one of the most dangerous operations, and safer hydraulic presses were used in the nineteenth century.*

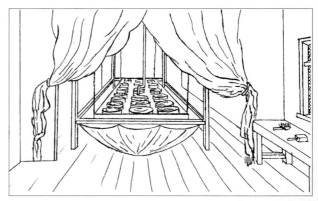

Above: *Front view of a corning machine, Faversham, 1796. Rows of sieves containing discs of lignum vitae, which break up the powder, are attached to a water-powered shaking frame. The sieves are double. The inner one is made of parchment with holes 1/8 inch (3 mm) in diameter, and the outer one is made of finer reel cloth, which retains the grain and allows the dust to pass through. The grain size of cannon powder, or large grain, was 8 to 16 meshes to the inch (25 mm) and that of musket powder, or fine grain, was 16 to 36.*

Left: *Slope reel for dusting, Faversham, 1796. Corned powder was loaded at the higher end and tumbled through the cylinder as it rotated. Remaining dust passed through the silk covering of the reel and was collected for reprocessing.*

GRANULATING MACHINE

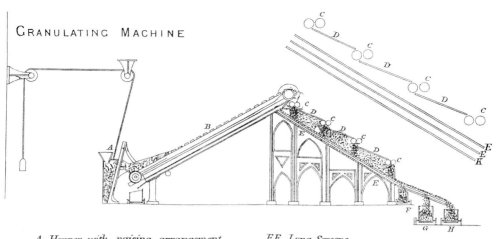

A. *Hopper with raising arrangement.*
B. *Endless band*
C.C.C.C. *Four pairs of rollers*
D.D.D. *Short screens.*

EE. *Long Screens*
F. *Box for dust*
G. *Box for grain*
H. *Box for chucks*
K. *Bottom board*

Above: *A nineteenth-century granulating machine. This type of machine, with pairs of toothed gunmetal rollers, was designed by William Congreve the younger in 1815. Press cake was cut and automatically sorted into grain, dust and chucks, which went through the process again. From Wardell's 'Handbook of Gunpowder and Guncotton', 1888.*

the early method of corning by hand was first mechanised and then replaced by a more modern process. Later granulating machines had toothed rollers that cut the press cake into pieces. After it was corned, remaining dust was removed by tumbling the powder in gauze-covered revolving cylinders.

GLAZING AND DRYING

Glazing the powder, by tumbling it in barrels, was practised from about 1680 onwards in order to round the grains and cause inferior ones to disintegrate. In the nineteenth century the process became more sophisticated with the use of black lead to coat the grains of powder and make them resistant to moisture.

Some kinds of powder were effectively

Left: *Glazing barrels at Waltham Abbey, late nineteenth century. The barrels were 5 feet (1.5 metres) long, and each held 400 pounds (180 kg) of powder. Some types of powder were tumbled for three or four hours at 34 revolutions per minute. Black lead was added towards the end of the process to coat the grains and make them moisture resistant.*

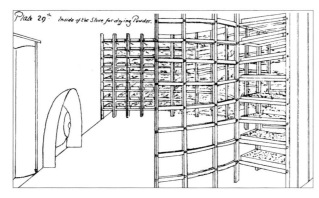

Plate 29ᵗʰ Inside of the Stove for drying Powder.

The interior of a gloom stove at Faversham, 1796. The powder was spread out to dry on the shelves, and the chamber was heated by the back of a cast-iron fireplace, shown on the left, which glowed red-hot. By this date gloom stoves were beginning to be replaced by safer stoves heated by steam pipes.

dried during glazing, but traditionally powder was dried in heated stoves or even in the open air. Early 'gloom' stoves were heated by a fireplace, but heating by steam pipes was introduced in the late eighteenth century. After it was dried, the powder was given a final dusting before being packed for distribution.

PROOF

Samples of gunpowder were regularly tested for quality and consistency by a variety of devices usually known by the French term *éprouvettes.* Vertical ratchet testers and pistol *éprouvettes* were in use in the seventeenth century. Other early methods used the distance of penetration of projectiles into clay or stacks of wooden boards, and another measured the range of cannonballs fired from a small mortar.

A breakthrough came in 1742 with the invention by Benjamin Robins of the ballistic pendulum, which enabled the muzzle velocity of projectiles to be measured with considerable accuracy. This provided a scientific basis on which to develop standards for the composition and grain size of gunpow-

A gunpowder proving pistol from the Battle powder mills in Sussex.

der. Electrical testers were developed in the nineteenth century. The most successful of these was the Boulengé chronograph, in which a projectile broke two wire screens a given distance apart.

PACKING AND TRANSPORT

Gunpowder was traditionally packed in oak barrels and kegs of various sizes, the 100 pound (44 kg) barrel being used as the standard unit of weight in marketing. Most powder mills had their own cooperage, and this employed a large proportion of the workforce. At the Roslin works in Midlothian in the 1840s, for instance, half the sixty employees were coopers. Small quantities of powder were sold in metal flasks and canisters, and products such as cartridges were packed in boxes.

For transport within factories, punts were used on millstreams wherever possible, and tramways were laid to connect the different buildings, with the trams pulled by

An advertising plaque (top right) from the Roslin mills, which operated from about 1805 to 1954, and a selection of packaging labels. Daye Barker & Co ran the Lowwood mills in Cumbria from 1798 to 1863; Kynoch Limited, ammunition manufacturers, took over the gunpowder works at Worsbrough Dale near Barnsley in 1893. The codes F, FF and FFF denote increasing grades of fineness.

horses or pushed by workmen.

Gunpowder was stored in factory magazines while awaiting dispatch. An Act of Parliament of 1772 required private firms to maintain magazines on the Thames below Blackwall or in other licensed places. Many of these warehouses were situated on the Thames estuary in Kent and Essex, and there were others at Bristol and Liverpool. The government factories had magazines at Purfleet in Essex, and an Act of 1851 provided for floating magazines to be established for the Ordnance on the Mersey at Liverpool.

Coopers of the Elterwater Gunpowder Company in the late nineteenth century. The Elterwater factory, which operated from 1824 to 1928, was one of a group in southern Cumbria that made blasting powder for home and export markets. Powder was delivered by horse and cart to the local Langdale slate quarries and Coniston copper mines and sent by rail to Liverpool for export, much of it to West Africa.

Carriage was at first by packhorse, and, as transport systems developed, wagons, canal barges and railways were in turn adopted. There was also a considerable coastal traffic in gunpowder. For transport inland, waterways provided a particularly suitable means of transport, and the government and several private firms maintained their own fleets of sailing barges.

EXPLOSIONS

Minor accidents were commonplace, and most mills would experience a fatal explosion occasionally. Fortunately the number of casualties was not usually large, in comparison with, for example, mining disasters, but details are invariably gruesome.

Most manufacturing accidents occurred in incorporating mills, but those in press and corning houses were more serious in terms of loss of life and injury. The worst were multiple accidents such as that at Kames in Argyll in 1863 in which a granulating house, press house, glazing house, dusting house, double press house and glazing house exploded in succession, killing seven men and injuring eight others.

Early legislation was concerned only with the needs of the state for supplies, and the first Act of Parliament to deal with public safety was that of 1719 which regulated the carriage of gunpowder in London and Westminster. Similar provisions were made for the rest of Great Britain in 1771, and the first Act to cover manufacturing practices was passed in the following year. This introduced manufacturing licences, prohibited pestle mills in general and limited the quantities of powder to be incorporated and dried at one time. It controlled the storage of powder and required magazines to be provided remote from the mills.

Safety measures involved taking steps to avoid bringing dust and grit into contact with gunpowder and guarding against sparks from iron objects and heat caused by friction. It became the practice to cover the floors of danger buildings with tanned

Packing gunpowder at the Oare works, Faversham, about 1925. Powder is being packed into flasks and canisters. The large labelled boxes contain blasting pellets.

Powder barges at Oare Creek, Faversham, about 1925. Powder was carried from the works to the wharf in the covered horse-drawn wagons on the left and taken by sailing barge to magazines on the Thames at Tilbury. The barges are flying the red flag to show they have explosives on board.

An explosion at the incorporating mills, Waltham Abbey, 1861. Workmen had neglected to place the customary piece of leather under the edge runners when they were being moved for cleaning, and a spark ignited the powder. Four men were badly burnt, and one of them died from his injuries. The picture shows a typical arrangement of six incorporating mills powered by a steam engine, in this case a beam engine in the tall engine house. A covered tram can be seen at the left of the picture.

hides and for the men to change into special slippers on entering. Copper and wooden utensils were used instead of iron, and copper was used for metal parts and fittings. When carrying powder, containers and wagons were covered with leather to prevent spillage. Danger buildings were surrounded on three sides with massive earth embankments and partially built of flimsy materials, to control the effect of any blast. Buildings were widely spaced to prevent explosions from spreading, and trees were used as shock absorbers.

However, although sound practices evolved, rules were not always observed. The next major legislation was passed in 1860 and was soon found to be inadequate, partly because it was overtaken by the development of new products, but also because of the difficulty of enforcing its provisions. A disastrous explosion of a magazine at Erith in Kent in 1864 highlighted the need for change. A subsequent report on the state of the Thames embankment in the area, where many magazines were situated, gave a startling account of careless attitudes and practices. A partial system of inspection and inquiry into major accidents was started and was later made comprehensive and permanent by the Explosives Act of 1875.

Meanwhile, in 1874, another salutary incident occurred when one of a convoy of five narrow boats, which was bound for the Midlands, exploded while passing beneath a bridge on the Regent's Canal in London. It was carrying a mixed cargo containing both gunpowder and benzolene, and vapour from the latter was ignited by a naked flame in the cabin.

The new Act introduced a list of authorised explosives and a licensing system for factories and stores based on the submission of detailed plans and the practice of inspection. In the field of transport, model codes of bylaws were prepared for the use of railway, canal and harbour companies. All accidents were required to be notified, and the number of deaths and injuries was substantially reduced. For the explosives industry as a whole, fatalities declined from forty-three per annum in England and Wales before 1870 to approximately seven per annum in the United Kingdom after 1878.

Powder punts on the millstream at Chilworth, Surrey, 1913. The leats of water-powered mills provided a convenient means of transport within factories. The photograph shows the leather covers on the barrels. These were used to prevent powder from being spilt.

THE FINAL PHASE

With advances in the design of guns in the second half of the nineteenth century, corresponding improvements were needed in the manufacture of powder for specific purposes. This was made possible by better methods of testing, which allowed greater control to be exercised over, for example, the properties of the charcoal used and the density of the finished product.

Slow-acting charges were needed both for rifled guns and for the heavy artillery that was made to penetrate armour plating on ships. The density of the powder was therefore increased, first by cutting press cake into ¹/₂ inch (13 mm) cubes instead of granulating it, to produce 'pebble powder', and later by using a hydraulic press or a cam press to mould powder into cylinders and prisms. Some products also had a reduced sulphur content to slow down combustion.

A problem with black powder was the amount of smoke it created, obscuring the target from view. To overcome this, an almost smokeless powder, known as brown prismatic or 'cocoa' powder, was produced by using brown charcoal made from straw.

Blasting charges were also made in the form of compacted 'bobbin powder', perforated cylinders of ³/₄ inch to 1¹/₂ inches (19 to 38 mm) in diameter which when in use were threaded on to lengths of fuse. A later product, 'bobbinite', was an adaptation of the black powder formula for use in coal mines where there was a risk of firedamp.

During the nineteenth century some firms began to expand, notably Curtis's &

Harvey's, which was established at Hounslow in 1820 and proceeded to take over other companies throughout the British Isles. The industry also acquired an international dimension when in 1885 a subsidiary of a German company took over the Chilworth works in Surrey for the manufacture of brown prismatic powder.

Meanwhile the modern high explosives industry had been undergoing rapid development. The new technology, which was based on the nitration of glycerine, cellulose and other organic compounds, had begun experimentally in Italy and Switzerland in the 1840s, and, after a protracted development stage, blasting agents had gone into regular production in the 1860s. The zenith of black powder technology was reached just as a breakthrough was being made in controlling the power of the new explosives for ballistic use.

The new products included dynamite, blasting gelatine and the propellant ballistite, all patented by the Swedish inventor Alfred Nobel, and the propellant cordite, which was developed under the auspices of the British government. Nobel set up companies to manufacture his products in several countries, and one of these, the British Dynamite Company, opened a factory at Ardeer on the Ayrshire coast in 1872.

Many existing gunpowder factories were redeveloped and extended to manufacture the new products. The manufacture of black powder ceased in Cornwall and Devon by the end of the nineteenth century, its end hastened by a slump in the mining industry. The explosives industry as a whole, however, expanded, with the workforce in the United Kingdom increasing from 7500 in the late 1870s to 14,500 at the end of the century. Dramatic expansion, on an international scale, occurred in the years leading up to the First World War of 1914-18. After the armistice, when demand suddenly fell, the successor of the British Dynamite Company arranged a merger of explosives firms in Britain. In the rationalisation that followed, most of the factories closed, and the manufacture of explosives became largely concentrated at Ardeer. The new company, Nobel Industries Limited, itself became part of Imperial Chemical Industries in 1926.

Black powder was still used for fuses and fireworks and for blasting in slate

Incorporating mills at Ballincollig, County Cork, photographed before the development of the site as a museum. The aerial view shows part of a row of twelve pairs of mills along the bank of the river Lee. Each pair has a central waterwheel pit and is separated from the next by a high blast wall with buttresses.

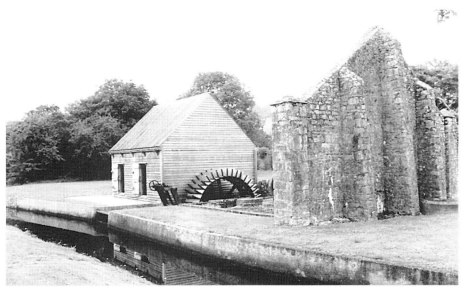

The Royal Gunpowder Mills Museum, Ballincollig, County Cork. The waterwheel and one of the pair of incorporating mills it drove have been reconstructed. A bedstone and a pair of edge runners are displayed on the foundations of the second mill, and the protective blast wall on its right has been conserved. The mill leat and the sluice to the waterwheel can be seen in the foreground. The mills were owned by the government from 1805 to 1833, and subsequent owners retained the name 'Royal'.

Interior of the reconstructed incorporating mill at Ballincollig, photographed at the official opening of the museum in 1993.

Above: *A saltpetre boiling pan in a garden at Battle, Sussex. The bowl is 52 inches (1.3 metres) in diameter and 33 inches (0.85 metre) deep. A similar pan can be seen at Hastings Museum.*

Right: *Charcoal cylinders at Gatebeck, Cumbria. The site of the Gatebeck factory, which closed in 1937, has been developed as a holiday caravan site, and the cylinders, which are approximately 8 feet (2.5 metres) long, have been erected as gate posts.*

Below: *A nineteenth-century press house at Waltham Abbey. The press was powered by a hydraulic pump driven by the waterwheel. The structure behind is a protective 'traverse'. This is oval in plan with walls tapering upwards and is filled with earth to absorb the blast from any explosion.*

Powdermills, Dartmoor. The chimney shaft was probably associated with the preparation of raw materials. The pairs of incorporating mills or 'wheel houses' in the background were served in turn by a long leat that carried water across the moor from the river East Dart.

The recovery of a powder barge from a canal at Waltham Abbey in 1994. River barges such as this were used to bring raw materials to the works and carry finished powder south down the Lee Navigation to government magazines at Purfleet and the Royal Laboratories at Woolwich on the Thames. Smaller barges and punts were used for transport within the works, which had 5 miles (8 km) of navigable waterways within its boundaries at the beginning of the twentieth century. The remains of seventeen barges have been discovered by archaeologists working on the site.

quarries, where it was favoured for its clean, heaving action. It continued to be made at Faversham in Kent and at several sites in the Lake District. In 1934, however, when the political situation in Europe was again deteriorating, the Faversham business was moved to Ardeer. The last of the Lake District mills, Gatebeck, closed in 1937. Production ceased at the government factory at Waltham Abbey when plant was destroyed by enemy action in the Second World War. It continued at Ardeer until 1976, with some processes being carried out at Roslin in Midlothian until 1954.

The gunpowder industry is still active, though subject to change, in many parts of the world. Manufacture continues in several countries in western Europe, including Switzerland, Germany, France and Italy, and in North America and Brazil. There is a continuing demand for black powder for blasting in stone, particularly slate, quarries. It is needed for priming charges, for fuses and fireworks, for blank cartridges, as used for example in historical re-enactments, and for use with antique firearms.

A typical street name in the vicinity of a gunpowder works. This example is near the site of the former Hounslow mills in Middlesex.

FURTHER READING

Since the first edition of this book appeared in 1986, much new work has been published and several detailed archaeological surveys of gunpowder sites have been carried out by government agencies. An inexpensive summary of the archaeology and history of sites in the British Isles is provided by *Gunpowder Mills Gazetteer* (Society for the Protection of Ancient Buildings, Wind and Watermill Section, 1988). Recent general works include: *Gunpowder: the History of an International Technology*, edited by B. J. Buchanan (University of Bath Press, 1996); G. I. Brown, *The Big Bang* (Sutton Publishing, 1998); W. D. Cocroft, *Dangerous Energy – the Archaeology of Gunpowder and Explosives Manufacture* (English Heritage, 2000).

Technology: W. H. Wardell, *Handbook of Gunpowder and Guncotton* (HMSO, 1888); O. Guttman, *The Manufacture of Explosives* (two volumes, Whittaker, 1895); E. M. Patterson, *Gunpowder Terminology and Incorporation* (Faversham Society, 1986); G. Crocker and K. R. Fairclough, 'The Introduction of Edge Runner Incorporating Mills in the British Gunpowder Industry', *Industrial Archaeology Review*, volume 20 (1998), 23–36.

History: J. Needham, *Science and Civilisation in China* (Cambridge University Press, 1986), volume 5, part 7, 509–16; *Victoria County History of Surrey* (Constable 1902–12), volume 2, 306–29; *The Rise and Progress of the British Explosives Industry* (Whittaker, 1909); J. West, *Gunpowder, Government and War in the Mid-Eighteenth Century* (Royal Historical Society/Boydell Press, 1991); W. J. Reader, *Imperial Chemical Industries: a History. Volume I: The Forerunners 1870–1926* (Oxford University Press, 1970); G. Kelleher, *Gunpowder to Guided Missiles: Ireland's War Industries* (J. F. Kelleher, Inniscarra, 1993) is relevant to the British Isles in general; D. Wood, *Powderbarge W. D.* (Society for Sailing Barge Research, revised edition 2000); *Gunpowder Mills: Documents of the Seventeenth and Eighteenth Centuries* (Surrey Record Society, volume 36, 2000).

Regional and local works include: *Oh! Ye had to be Careful: Personal Recollections by Roslin Gunpowder Mill and Bomb Factory Workers*, edited by Ian MacDougall (Tuckwell Press, 2000); J. Robertson, 'The Powder Mills of Argyll', *Industrial Archaeology Review*, volume 12, number 2 (1990), 205–15; E. M. Patterson, 'The Explosion at Furnace', *Scots Magazine*, October 1968, 13–17; J. D. Marshall and M. Davis-Shiel, *The Industrial Archaeology of the Lake Counties* (Michael Moon, second edition 1977); E. M. Patterson, *Blackpowder Manufacture in Cumbria* (Faversham Society, 1995); J. Winfield, *The Gunpowder Mills of Fernilee*, published by the author (Whaley Bridge, Derbyshire), 1996; A. and G. Crocker, 'The Gunpowder Mills at Tyddyn Gwladdys, near Dolgellau', *Melin* (Welsh Mills Society), volume 12 (1996), 2–25; T. Pritchard, J. Evans and S. Johnson, *The Old Gunpowder Factory at Glynneath* (Merthyr Tydfil & District Naturalists' Society, 1985); B. Earl, *Cornish Explosives* (Trevithick Society, 1978); A. Pye, 'An Example of a Non-Metalliferous Dartmoor Industry', in *The Archaeology of Dartmoor*, edited by D. Griffiths, Devon Archaeological Society and Dartmoor National Park Authority, 1996, 221–40; B. J. Buchanan and M. T. Tucker, 'The Manufacture of Gunpowder: a Study of the Documentary and Physical Evidence relating to the Woolley Powder Works near Bath', *Industrial Archaeology Review*, volume 5, number 3 (1981), 185–202; P. Philo and J. Mills, 'The Bedfont Gunpowder Mills', *London Archaeologist*, volume 5 (1985), 95–102; K. Fairclough, 'Early Gunpowder Production at Waltham', *Essex Journal*, volume 20 (1985), 11–16; G. and A. Crocker, 'Gunpowder Mills of Surrey', *Surrey History*, volume 4, number 3 (1990), 134–58, and *Damnable Inventions: Chilworth Gunpowder and the Paper Mills of the Tillingbourne* (Surrey Industrial History Group, 2000); A. J. Percival, *The Faversham Gunpowder Industry and Its Development* (Faversham Society, third edition 1986); H. Blackman, 'The Story of the Old Gunpowder Works at Battle', *Sussex Archaeological Collections*, volume 64 (1923), 109–22.

Much detailed information is contained in reports of HM Inspectorate of Explosives, published in *Parliamentary Papers* from 1875 onwards.

Further information may be obtained from Dr B. J. Buchanan, Gunpowder and Explosives History Group, c/o Centre for the History of Technology, School of Social Sciences, University of Bath, Bath BA2 7AY.

PLACES TO VISIT

Intending visitors are advised to check the current status of museums and their opening times before making a special journey. Please note that on sites with informal access permission may be required to visit and ruined structures may be unsafe. Note also that the term 'gunpowder' has been used for propellants other than black powder made from saltpetre, charcoal and sulphur. Some sites known as gunpowder mills, for example at Fritham in the New Forest, are therefore outside the scope of this book.

MUSEUMS IN THE UNITED KINGDOM
Chart Gunpowder Mill, off Stonebridge Way, Faversham, Kent (restored incorporating mill). Enquiries to the Fleur de Lis Heritage Centre, telephone: 01795 534542. Website: www.faversham.org
Explosion – Museum of Naval Firepower, Priddy's Hard, Gosport, Hampshire PO12 4LE. Telephone: 023 9250 5678. Website: www.explosion.org.uk
Purfleet Heritage and Military Centre, Centurion Way, Purfleet, Essex RM19 1ZZ. Telephone: 01708 866764. Website: www.purfleet5.freeserve.co.uk/heritage.htm
Royal Gunpowder Mills, Beaulieu Drive, Waltham Abbey, Essex EN9 1JY. Telephone: 01992 767022. Website: www.royalgunpowdermills.com

MUSEUMS IN OTHER COUNTRIES
Denmark. The gunpowder factory at Frederiksvaerk, Sjaelland, is preserved as a museum but in 2002 is closed.
France. Sevran-Livry (15 km north-east of Paris). Nobel's house, public park and explosives museum on the site of the former Poudrerie Nationale. Telephone: (33) 1 49 36 51 75.
Greece. The Open-Air Water Power Museum of Dimitsana, Peloponnese, is an industrial complex including gunpowder mills. Telephone/fax: (30) 7950-31630.
Ireland. Ballincollig Gunpowder Mills, Ballincollig Regional Park, Co. Cork. Heritage Centre. Telephone: (353) 214 874430. Website: http:/indigo.ie/~ballinco
Portugal. Fábrica da Pólvora de Barcarena (10 km west of Lisbon). Site with industrial remains, developed as an arts and science complex. Telephone: (351) 214 408 553.
Tasmania. Penny Royal Gunpowder Mills, Launceston (reconstruction).
USA. Hagley Museum, Wilmington, Delaware 19807. Telephone: (302) 658 2400 extension 259. Website: www.hagley.lib.de.us

INDUSTRIAL ARCHAEOLOGY
Brief details of over eighty sites are given in the *Gunpowder Mills Gazetteer.* Those with more substantial remains or easy access are listed here.
Sites open as public amenities are Roslin (south of Edinburgh at National Grid Reference NT 268627), the Hounslow mills in Crane Park, Middlesex (TQ 129729), and part of the Chilworth site in Surrey (TQ 024475). Excavated remains can be seen on a riverside walk at Dartford, Kent (TQ 548730), and remains at Bedfont in Middlesex can be seen from a public footpath leading north from Baber Bridge (TQ 112746). There are plans to provide public access to the site of the Oare works (TR 003624) at Faversham in Kent. In East Sussex, remains at Battle (TQ 742146) and Sedlescombe (TQ 781176) are in private gardens; those at Sedlescombe and a dam at Peppering-Eye (TQ 743139) are visible from public footpaths. Kennall Vale in Cornwall (SW 750375) is managed as a nature reserve. Remains on Dartmoor are visible from a footpath from Higher Cherry Brook Bridge (SX 635770) but are on private land and permission is required to visit; a proving mortar stands by the approach to Powder Mills Farm (SX 627768). In Wales, there are public footpaths through the Glyn Neath site in West Glamorgan (SN 911080); remains of the Tyddyn Gwladys mills (SH 735270) are on private land but can be seen from the track to the Gwynfynnydd Gold Mines operated by the Welsh Gold Centre in Dolgellau. In western Scotland, there are substantial remains on private land at Clachaig (NS 120814), Furnace (NN 022005) and Kames, Kyles of Bute (NR 958707).
The following are used as holiday accommodation, and non-residents must obtain permission to visit: Sedgwick (SD 508877), Gatebeck (SD 544855) and Lowwood (SD 348837) in Cumbria are caravan parks; Elterwater in Cumbria (NY 327052) and Melfort in Argyll (NM 840145) are time-share developments; Herodsfoot in Cornwall (SX 205608) is occupied by Deerpark Forest Cabins.